Chalk Painting 101: Upcycle Furniture and Home Décor in 10 Easy Steps

Robyn Clemens, Ed. S

This book or any portion thereof may not be reproduced or used in any manner whatsoever without the express written permission of the publisher except for the use of brief quotations in a book review.

Although the author has made every effort to ensure that the information in this book is correct, the author does not assume and hereby disclaim any liability to any party for any loss, damage, or disruption caused by errors or omissions, whether such errors or omissions result from negligence, accident, or any other cause.

CONTENTS

INTRODUCTION

You can't browse a decorating magazine, renovation show or DIY blog without spotting dreamy chalk painted furniture and home décor. Fueled by the trending farmhouse, French country, and coastal styles, the chalk painting craze just keeps booming. My mission in this book is to help you develop the confidence you need to tackle your first chalk paint project, instead of just admiring the work of others. If you have already experienced the thrill of upcycling with chalk paint, this book will offer easy tips to simplify the painting process. The before and after pictures of my favorite projects will inspire you to look beyond the surface and imagine many more chalk painted creations.

I know what you're thinking, "I'm no artist and chalk painting sounds too advanced for my newbie skills." Well, nothing could be farther from the truth. As a matter of fact, chalk paint is the perfect medium for beginners because there's no need to sand, strip, or prime your piece before painting it. That's right-no prep work! Trust me, if you're longing to create easy, one-of-a-kind home decor, chalk paint is your answer!

As an art teacher, I know how intimidating it can be to get started, so I will paint a piece right along with you. I will guide you through easy-to-follow steps using how-to photos, so you can transform your dreary find into a masterpiece.

Step 1: Understanding Chalk Paint

When I began reading about restoring furniture with chalk paint, I have to admit I was a little skeptical. A low odor, water based paint that required no prep sounded too good to be true. For years, I had successfully upcycled my furniture and home décor using latex paint, even though I wasn't a fan of the labor intensive process. Since latex paint doesn't adhere well to some surfaces, I was forced to apply a primer as a base coat before I could even begin to paint. In addition, some pieces required stripping and sanding which was even more time consuming. By the time I finished all the prep work, I was too tired to paint my piece, and would postpone it until the next day.

Latex paint can also be problematic for those suffering with asthma and allergies. The paint, as well as the products used to seal it, can produce irritating fumes. As an asthma sufferer, this was a major drawback for me.

Finally, I decided there must be a faster and easier way to create stylish pieces for my home so I started reading about the benefits of chalk paint. In spite of my reservations, I eventually bought my first quart of chalk paint and decided to give it a go. All I had to do now was find my next paint project.

As fate would have it, the following week I ran across an unfinished farmhouse table at my favorite thrift store. The moment I saw it, I knew it could be upcycled with a little love, so I coaxed my sweet husband into loading it in our pick up and we were on our way. The next day, I finally opened that first quart of chalk paint and started transforming my drab table.

My inspiration for the table came from a pricey online version that was completely out of my budget, so I set out to make may own on the cheap. The online table had a dark wood top and chalk painted legs. I decided to mimic the style by staining the top and chalk painting only the table legs and apron. Chalk painting requires no prep, so I simply wiped away the dust and started painting the legs right away. No stripping, sanding, or priming! I have to admit, I was shocked by how much easier it was.

Unfortunately, the table top wasn't quite as simple. Since I chose to stain it, I had to sand it down, apply the stain, let it dry, and finally seal it with polyurethane. Whew! What a process! At that moment I realized how much more enjoyable the chalk painting process had been and I was hooked!

{My farmhouse table before and after}

It all worked out in the end, and I was able to transform my thrift store table into a statement piece. My first chalk paint project was a huge success and all I could think was, "Chalk paint, where have you been all my life?"

The farmhouse table ended up being the first chalk painted piece I ever sold. I used my profits to purchase a lot more chalk paint, wax, and my first good wax brush. The idea that I could make money doing something I loved to do, intrigued me. The best part was I could cheaply update furniture for my own home using the same products.

The first year, I chalk painted dozens of neglected pieces and even sold some of my thrifted finds in order to restock my supply of chalk paint. When I started sharing my before and after pictures, people began hiring me to do home renovation projects like painting fireplaces and bathroom cabinets.

As an artist, I'm not surprised by the popularity of chalk paint. It's now my favorite upcycling medium because it can be applied to almost any surface, including wood, plastic, metal, and fabric without priming! As a matter of fact, I have yet to find a surface I couldn't chalk paint!

I absolutely love that chalk paint is a water based product, with easy cleanup and no strong fumes. Chalk paint requires NO previous painting experience and is super easy to apply. I promise you will love this product. Your only regret will be that you didn't try it sooner!

Here are a few more before and after pictures that I hope will inspire you to start painting:

{Blue chalk paint revives this tired bathroom vanity}

{This cabinet was my first paid chalk painting job!}

Thrifting is my jam, so every project you see in this book was upcycled using salvaged, thrifted, or hand-me-down pieces. I'm *always* on the lookout for neglected furniture and home décor in need of restoration.

I rescued this side table from my neighbor's yard sale. She said she bought it for a project but never got around to painting it. Lucky me! Just like the farm table, I could see the potential in this piece. It had great bones, so I knew it could be saved. It was definitely worth the $10 I paid for it!

{This piece makes me happy every time I see it!}

Once you start chalk painting, be on the lookout for treasures you can upcycle as well. If you aren't into thrifting, put the word out to family and friends and you will be amazed by how many cool pieces appear at your door step. People give me stuff all the time because they know I will turn it into something unique.

It may sound degrading, but I've even been known to pick up pieces from roadside trash. I once scavenged an old oil painting from my neighbor's driveway. When I called her up and asked if I could have it for a project she replied, "Sure, but I know you're going to turn it into something beautiful!" A few months later, she came by my house and happened to compliment the custom painted chalkboard in my entry. When I told her it was made from her trashed frame, she said, "I just knew you were going to turn it into something great!"

Keep watching out for pieces that can be repurposed or spruced up with a little chalk paint. You'll be shocked at the number of treasures you'll find. If dumpster diving isn't your thing, "shop" your home for cool pieces to upcycle for free. We all have items collecting dust that can be brought back to life with a little chalk paint.

Tip #1: Start small, build your confidence, and then go bigger. It's that easy!

My "trash to treasure" chalkboard is still a big hit at family gatherings and the best part is I can customize it to any occasion. In this picture, we used it to welcome guests to our annual Fourth of July celebration. My daughter even displayed it at her wedding reception to post the seating chart. It was much more sentimental than a store bought sign.

In the next few pages, you will see more home décor pieces I restored using chalk paint. Most of the items were hand-me-downs or thrifted finds costing $10 dollars or less. Before you read on, take a minute to start thinking about items you'd like to upcycle.

Step 2- Finding Your Piece

I have discovered that most people are a little intimidated by chalk paint in the beginning, so I wouldn't risk overwhelming yourself with a large furniture project. Instead, build your confidence by choosing a small, easy to paint piece, which will give you a sense of accomplishment right away.

Here's a list of good starter pieces for beginners:

- Mirrors
- Chairs
- Side tables
- Trunks
- Chests
- Bookshelves
- Benches
- Candlesticks
- Picture frames
- Sofa tables
- Dressers
- Plant stands

This adorable accent chair started out as a dated seventies cast off. A little creamy white chalk paint and $10 fabric transformed it into my favorite reading chair.

Reupholstering can be expensive, so I bartered with a friend who agreed to do it at half the price! The green metal plant stand was once a drab, hunter green hand-me-down. Now, it has a fresh pop of color that cheers up any room in my house.

{It's fun to paint functional pieces like this ladder}

The little bench had an outdated cherry finish and a worn cushion. Soft gray chalk paint and $1 fabric remnant brought it back to life.

I enjoy repurposing salvaged wood scraps. This jewelry display was made using chalk paint and ceramic knobs. Since I already had left over paint from a previous job, the entire project only cost $8 to make. It's one of my favorites because it serves a function in my home while looking fabulous! You might consider painting functional pieces like picture frames or bookshelves for your first project since they don't take much time to complete.

Do you happen to have an old trunk collecting dust in your home? I scored this one at a garage sale for just $10! I wasn't a fan of the color so I perked it up with turquoise chalk paint. I love the distressed look and it makes a really unique décor piece, especially during the holidays!

Step 3- Selecting Your Workspace

After many years of painting both indoors and outside, I've discovered I prefer to paint inside. Painting indoors allows me to have control over my painting environment, especially the temperature of the room. It didn't take me long to realize chalk paint dries quickly so it's not a good idea to paint in extreme temperatures.

I also recommend leaving fans off during painting. In my experience, a fan dries out the paint too quickly, making application more difficult. I only use a fan when I'm trying to dry my project *after* it has been painted.

Lighting is the next external factor to consider when choosing a workspace. You want as much natural light as possible, as well as task lighting, especially when waxing and buffing. We will address those stages in Steps 8 and 9.

Lastly, protect your surfaces from paint splatter and drips by covering them with a drop cloth or paper.

Tip# 2: Drop cloths can be pricey, so I don't buy them. Instead, I use a flat plastic table cover with cotton backing. It wipes clean and the backing allows you to easily turn your piece while you're painting to reach all areas. If you don't have one of these on hand, a flat sheet works great as well.

Step 4- Choosing Chalk Paint

There are many brands of chalk paint out there which can be a little confusing. You can find dozens of options at big box retailers and online. Craft and hobby stores often carry their own line of chalk paint as well. Some brands are pricey, but keep in mind, a little product goes a long way. After testing several kinds over the years, I've discovered I usually get what I pay for. Meaning, the cheaper brands aren't always a good deal in the end. Some less expensive brands don't seem to cover as well as their more expensive counterparts.

I prefer to use a higher quality chalk paint and have never been disappointed with my results. I usually end up using less paint because the coverage is so much better. I recently finished 6 projects with just one quart of high quality chalk paint!

If your funds are very limited, you might consider creating your own chalk paint by adding water to one part plaster of Paris and three parts latex paint. However, in this book we're focused on chalk painting the *easy* way. Making your own paint adds several steps to the process so you might want to hold off until you feel you've mastered the medium.

Wax is also a wonderful, easy to apply product that I use on all my pieces. I love how smooth the finish becomes after the wax is applied. Like paint, wax comes in a variety of colors. In the beginning, I used basic clear wax on every project. When I became more comfortable with the application process, I worked my way up to the more intimidating dark, white, and black waxes.

Some chalk paint brands can only be purchased through retailers called "stockists" but if there isn't one near you, shipping is an option. I have also found several chalk paint products at my local craft retailer that will certainly do the job. The important thing is to buy your paint so you can get started!

Tip#3: What if your color isn't just right? When I buy chalk paint, I always buy white and black of the same brand. That way, if I'm not satisfied with the color, I can change it easily by adding white to make a lighter tint or black to create a darker shade of the original color.

Step 5- Gathering Supplies

You will need the following:
- ✓ Chalk paint
- ✓ Paint brush
- ✓ Sand paper
- ✓ Clear wax
- ✓ Wax brush or cloth
- ✓ Paint stick
- ✓ Paper plate
- ✓ Plastic spoon
- ✓ Screwdriver
- ✓ Drop cloth or table cover
- ✓ Paper towels

*Optional Items:
- ✓ New hardware
- ✓ Medicine dropper
- ✓ Baby wipes (for easy cleanup)
- ✓ Painter's tape
- ✓ Plastic wrap or foil

Step 6- Preparing to Paint

I've already mentioned that chalk paint requires no stripping, sanding, or priming. However, there are a few easy things you should always do before you begin a project.

First, take a quick "before" picture of your project. It's rewarding to look back on a piece you've reimagined and compare the original to your newly transformed version. Here's my before pic of the piece I'm painting along with you today:

{Picked up this cutie at a yard sale for 5 bucks!}

{Talk about your easy prep!}

Remove any drawers, hardware, or shelves before painting. If your piece has any nail holes or deep scratches, you could use wood filler to cover them. I think dings and marks bring character to a piece and add to the "worn over time" vibe, so I prefer to leave them. As the artist, it's totally your call.

You should always cover work surfaces, including floors, to protect them from stray paint and spills. Next, wipe the piece down using mild soap and water, or a baby wipe. This will ensure you have a clean surface, free of dust and grime. Let it dry completely before you paint.

Step 7- Let's Paint!

I know the first brush stroke is the scariest, so I'm going to walk you through it. Some people complain that chalk paint can be a little "streaky" but I've never found that to be a problem. From the first brush stroke, I was amazed by the buttery feel and easy coverage. My guess is the complaints stem from the fact that chalk paint is thicker than latex. Chalk paint is formulated to have a more textured feel than other paints. It's not supposed to be completely smooth.

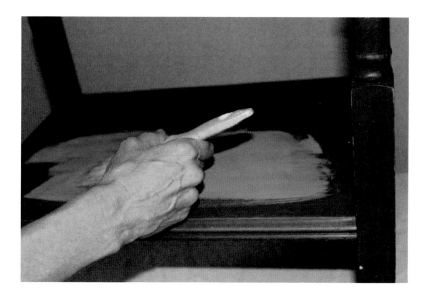

If you like texture, you can create even more by brushing in different directions.

Tip#4: If your paint isn't gliding on as smoothly as you would like, add a few drops of water and you should see a big improvement. I like to use a medicine dropper for this. It's easy to dispense and it keeps you from adding too much water.
{Hint: My local pharmacy gives them away for free!}

Chalk paint is very forgiving, so there's no need to worry about your paint technique, even if you've never painted before. Remember, if you want a smoother finish, try painting in the same direction using even strokes to avoid drips and runs. If you are going for an aged, textured look, brush in all directions allowing the paint to accumulate unevenly. The paint is designed to show texture, so don't worry when you see brush marks-I promise you will love it in the end!

Tip# 5: If you've selected a wood piece, and desire an even finish, try painting with the grain of the wood to reduce streaking.

Your goal on your first coat is to simply cover the piece entirely. It's fine if some spots are covered more than others. You can see in the pictures (right), that my brush marks are quite noticeable. I envisioned a smooth, creamy texture for my table so I decided to add a second coat. This should hide most my brush marks.

{My table after one coat of chalk paint}

{Brush marks are normal, so don't stress!}

Tip #6: Wrapping your paint brush in aluminum foil or plastic will keep it from drying out between coats.

Let the first coat of paint dry for around 20 minutes. You can leave the piece as it is, or you can apply a second coat. A second coat will even out the coverage and eliminate any imperfections you may have noticed after your first coat. If you're going for an aged look, you may decide one coat is enough.

When you are satisfied with the coverage, take a few minutes to look at your piece closely for spots you may have missed. I like to turn it over checking all angles before I clean my brush. There's nothing more frustrating than washing out your paint brush only to find you missed a spot later.

Now, clean out your brush, removing all paint.

Tip#7: Always let your brush dry, bristle side up, before storing it way.

Let the paint dry thoroughly. Drying time varies by product and painting conditions. The beauty of chalk paint is it dries quickly, so you don't have to wait long before going on. When your paint is dry to the touch, you're good to go on to step 8, applying wax.

Step 8- Applying Wax

When I started to research chalk painting techniques years ago, I noticed some debate over *when* to wax. Some artists suggested waxing before distressing, while others insisted distressing should be done before applying wax. Let me say, I've done it both ways but I prefer to wax first then distress. I follow up with another thin coat of wax to add a little extra protection from wear.

You're going to love wax because it brings out the very faint details in your piece, making them more prominent. This step is critical if you want your piece to remain as you painted it. Without a protective topcoat, chalk paint wears off in exposed areas over time.

However, if you like the vintage, chippy look, you may choose to skip the wax altogether. Personally, I think waxed pieces are more durable and have a richer, more finished quality. Wax is not only a protective seal, but also a finishing agent that works to smooth your surface.

Tip#8: Wax is your friend, don't be afraid to use it!

I will warn you, some beginners shy away from chalk paint because they are afraid of the waxing process. There's no need to worry, waxing is much easier than it sounds. As a matter of fact, if you can properly apply hand lotion, you can apply wax! Think of it like this, you would never apply hand lotion without rubbing it in completely. The same method applies to wax. Whether applying with a brush or a cloth, make sure you rub it in and wipe off the excess. To quote one of my favorite 80's movies, "Wax on, wax off!" Applied correctly, wax will smooth out your finish and add another layer of depth and interest.

If your paint is *completely* dry, you're ready to try wax. First, you need to scoop out a small spoonful of clear wax and place it on a paper plate. Dab your wax brush (or cloth) in the wax and rub it around on the plate. Your goal is to evenly coat your brush with a *small* amount of wax before applying it. Using light pressure, move over a section of your piece, rubbing in a circular motion. Focus on only a small area, wiping away the excess as you go along. Move on to the next section, repeating the process until your entire piece has a light coat of wax. A little wax goes a long way, so don't use too much.

Tip# 9: Your piece should not feel tacky, if it does you need to remove the excess wax with a cloth.

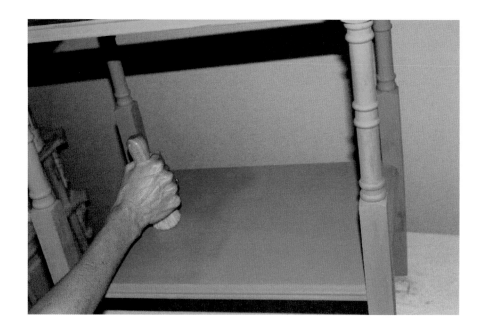

{Apply the wax with a brush or cloth, using a circular motion}

Remember what I told you about your wax finish- it's not permanent. With heavy use, it can start to wear down. So, as much as I love wax, there are times when I choose to use a more permanent sealer like a water based topcoat. If your piece is going to be used in a high traffic area, you might consider this option.

{My table with just half of the wax applied}

I love how waxing makes the paint look richer and more polished. It also brings out the subtle textures and characteristics of each piece. In the picture above, you can see the contrast between the waxed side (left) and the unwaxed side (right). Wax makes a big difference and the super silky feel is an added bonus.

I like to wait 24 hours before using one of my chalk painted pieces. This gives the wax time to start the curing process.

Step 9- Distressing

Finally, you have a painted and waxed piece! Congrats on a job well done! When the wax dries, you have the option of adding character to your piece by distressing it. This simply means you can use sand paper to remove some of the paint to accentuate the lines and details of your piece. This step is completely optional, but it can give your piece a more finished look, so I usually recommend it. There are many methods of distressing, but I believe sanding is the easiest by far.

{I decided to lightly sand this piece.}

{Distressing accentuates the lines in this piece}

When I choose to distress, I use fine or medium grit sand paper to sand away areas that would naturally be exposed to wear, like corners, sides, and edges. I usually start sanding on a spot that is not noticeable, like the back of the piece. That way, I can get a feel for how much I want to sand away before moving on to the parts that actually show. If I decide heavy distressing is needed, I use a course grit sand paper because it removes the paint faster. I usually finish off the sanded parts with a little more wax.

Tip#10: The level of distressing really depends on the look and feel you want for your piece.

{Close up look at my distressed side table}

If the idea of distressing is making you a little nervous, practice on a small piece of painted molding or wood scrap to perfect your skills. The first time I tried it, I used a free paint stick from the hardware store because I was afraid I would ruin my piece.

Since there are different levels of distressing, it's a good idea to think back to the vision you had for your piece before you started painting it. If you imagined a worn, vintage vibe, heavy distressing might be for you. Heavily sanded pieces take on an aged, time-worn appearance. I wanted a more polished look for my table, so I decided to lightly distress it with fine grit sandpaper. If you happen to have a power sander, I wouldn't recommend using it. Distressing is a subtle effect which is easiest to achieve with hand sanding.

Step 10- Buffing

One step you don't hear a lot about is buffing. If you finished waxing and you want your piece to have a more polished look, you can buff it with a lint free cloth until you have a nice sheen.

Even though wax dries very quickly, it will take 5 to 20 days for it to completely cure. Once it has cured, it will have an extremely durable, satin finish. For an extra smooth finish, wait until your piece has cured and buff it again.

{My finished table-What a transformation!}

It's time to show off your skills!

Well, you did it! I have to say, this is by far the most rewarding part of the chalk painting process. It's time to take a minute to admire all of your hard work. Remember the "before" picture you took of your piece? Study that picture so you can recall what it looked like when you started this project.

Now take the "after" picture of your newly transformed treasure and celebrate your accomplishment! You just created a one-of-a-kind work of art! That's a pretty big deal! Show it off to your friends, post it on social media, and proudly bask in the glow of your awesomeness!

I promised at the beginning of this book to help you start small, grow in confidence, and go bigger. I hope I have achieved my mission, because I believe you have many more amazing transformations ahead of you. Congratulations! You now have the skills you need to complete all of your furniture and home décor projects. Don't forget to "shop" your home and make a list of future projects you'd like to upcycle.

You're ready to go BIG!

Acknowledgements

Thank you Lord for your unending blessings and for giving me the strength to do all things.
{Philippians 4:13}
To my amazing husband and best friend whose love has always given me confidence to dream big-God knew my heart needed you!
To my talented children, Lauren, Caleb, Gracie, and Ellie-I'm blessed to be your Mom and I'll love you forever!
Special thanks to Amy at Thrift Fabrics for making my visions a reality and to my photography assistant, Ellie Jean, whose persistence helped me finish this project.

About the Author

Robyn Clemens is a chalk paint artist and master educator with over 25 years of teaching experience. The grandmother and mom of four lives in Mt. Washington, Kentucky with her children and husband. She currently teaches art in a small Kentucky town. Some people only dream of meeting their favorite artists, Robyn teaches hers every day!

Made in the
USA
Monee, IL